Blue Earth

Other Books by Aliki Barnstone

Poetry

The Real Tin Flower
Windows in Providence
Madly in Love
Wild With It

Anthologies

A Book of Women Poets from Antiquity to Now
with Willis Barnstone
The Calvinist Roots of the Modern Era
with Michael Manson & Carol J. Singely
The Shambhala Anthology of Women's Spiritual Poetry
(paperback edition of *Voices of Light:
Spiritual and Visionary Poems by Women
Around the World from Ancient Sumeria to Now*)

Edition

Trilogy by H.D.
Introduction and Readers' Notes by Aliki Barnstone

Blue Earth

poems

Aliki Barnstone

Iris Press
Oak Ridge, Tennessee

Copyright © 2004 by Aliki Barnstone

All rights reserved. No portion of this book may be reproduced in any form or by any means, including electronic storage and retrieval systems, without explicit, prior written permission of the publisher, except for brief passages excerpted for review and critical purposes.

Cover Photo:
Copyright © 2004 by Joseph Enzweiler

Author Photo:
Copyright © 2004 by Stephen Davis

Font:
Minion

Design:
Robert B. Cumming, Jr.

Library of Congress Cataloging-in-Publication Data

Barnstone, Aliki.
 Blue earth : poems by Aliki Barnstone.
    p. cm.
 ISBN 0-916078-59-0 (pbk. : alk. paper)
 I. Title.
 PS3552.A72B55 2004
 811'.54—dc22

2004002757

Acknowledgments

Grateful acknowledgment is made to the journals in which the following poems have appeared, often in different form.

Agni: "A Declining Neighborhood"
Antioch Review: "On the Hottest San Francisco Day in Recorded History He Plays Piano and She Listens"
Artful Dodge: "Blue Room, Blue Horse"
Berkeley Poetry Review: "Sensual Pleasure That Is Achieved Morbidly, Corruptingly"
Caffeine Destiny (www.caffeinedestiny.com): "In the New Year," "Walking to Work in Milwaukee," "Spring Flick"
Chicago Review: "Spirals"
Colorado Review: "On the Ship"
Crab Orchard Review: "Seen from my Window in San Francisco"
Exquisite Corpse (paper): "The Cypress Tress of Mount Pelion," "Days of 1976" (as "Floating Through Austin with Liz")
Exquisite Corpse (online): "Green Shoes," "More than a Month of Gray Winter in Madison," "The Ferry to Serifos," "Anemos," "A Windy Night of Terror on Serifos," "Go to the Good and Return with the Good"
The Graham House Review: "Brothers"
Green Mountains Review: "Rowing on Lake Mendota"
Luna: "Cavafy in the Early Morning"
The Malahat Review: "Blue Earth," "Counting Time on Kímolos"
New England Review: "Sadness"
New Letters: "A Night in Rome"
ONTHEBUS: "At a Truckstop in Gyantse, Tibet"
Partisan Review: "The Irises of the Midwest"
Prairie Schooner: "Street Names," "Greek Easter," "The Bell"
Red Rock Review: "What's the Matter?" "Sun Fields in Tibet"
The Southern Review: "The Dog," "Portokali"
TriQuarterly: "Dream with Billie Holiday"
Witness: "First Memory in Nova Scotia," "The Black Room"

"Winter and War on Lake Monona" appeared in *A Glass of Green Tea With Honig*, edited by Susan Brown, Thomas Epstein, & Henry Gould. (Providence, RI: Apephoe Books, 1994).

I am grateful to the artists that produced several of these poems as collaborations with other media. "On the Hottest San Francisco Day in Recorded History He Plays Piano and She Listens" was recorded with my voice and Frank Haney on keyboards. Robert Barnstone made several of the poems in this book part of his sculptural installation, "The Narrative Forest."

Thank you to Edwin Honig, my early friend and teacher, for showing me the ways of discipline, formal play, and freedom, and for reading this book's first incarnation—*Estás simpre en mi córazon*. For their keen attention to this book, I thank my wonderful readers, Tony Barnstone, Willis Barnstone, Ralph Black, Tim Fuller, Cynthia Hogue, Alan Michael Parker, and Mark Turpin. To Robert Pinsky, for his loyal support and his help with some of these poems, I give abiding gratitude and admiration. I am grateful to Beth, whose warmth sheltered in the zeros in Madison, to my mother for giving me Greece and her painter's eye, and to Joseph and Zoë for giving love, hope, sanctuary, home.

For my father,
Willis Barnstone

Contents

Tibet

Sky Burial ~ 15
At a Truckstop in Gyantse, Tibet ~ 18
Sun Fields in Tibet ~ 19

Blue Room, Blue Horse

Blue Room, Blue Horse ~ 23
First Memory in Nova Scotia ~ 25
Spirals ~ 26
Street Names ~ 28
Spring Flick ~ 30
The Black Room ~ 31
Days of 1976 ~ 33
A Declining Neighborhood ~ 35
Seen from my Window in San Francisco ~ 37
What's the Matter? ~ 39
Sadness ~ 41
The Dog ~ 42
Jack's Defeat Creek ~ 44
On the Hottest San Francisco Day in Recorded History
He Plays Piano and She Listens ~ 45

Blue Earth

Blue Earth ~ 49
In the New Year ~ 51
Winter and War on Lake Monona ~ 53
More Than a Month of Gray Winter in Madison ~ 55
Dream with Billie Holiday ~ 57
Walking to Work in Milwaukee ~ 59
Green Shoes ~ 61
The Irises of the Midwest ~ 63
Rowing on Lake Mendota ~ 64

The Ferry To Serifos

Cavafy in the Early Morning ∾ 67
The Cypress Trees of Mount Pelion ∾ 68
Greek Easter ∾ 69
Brothers ∾ 71
The Ferry to Serifos ∾ 73
Anemos ∾ 74
A Windy Night of Terror on Serifos ∾ 75
Counting Time on Kímolos ∾ 76
Portokali ∾ 78
A Night in Rome ∾ 80
The Bell ∾ 83
Pleasure Attained Morbidly, Harmfully ∾ 86
On The Ship ∾ 88
Go to the Good and Return with the Good ∾ 89

Notes ∾ 92

Think of the long trip home.
Should we have stayed at home and thought of here?
Where should we be today?

—Elizabeth Bishop, from "Questions of Travel"

Ithaka gave you the beautiful journey.
Without her you would not have set out on the way.
She has no more to give you.

And if you find her poor, Ithaka did not betray you.
With all your knowledge, all your experience,
you understand by now what Ithakas mean.

—C.P. Cavafy, from "Ithaka"

Tibet

Sky Burial

Snowlands Hotel. Before dawn in one of the dormitories
David is up first, moving from bed to bed waking us gently.
We mount our clanky Flying Pigeon bikes and ride out of town

on the dusty road, telling each other our dreams.
Travelers' word is if a fire's burning there will be a burial.
The fire burns. We park our bicycles by a shallow river

and roll up our pants to cross. Water so icy that I bend over
on the opposite shore, breathing slowly, coaxing my feet
from their pain. Already the vultures' silhouettes gather

on the mountain above us. A monk in yellow robes
bright in the dim light chants, hits a tambourine and cymbal.
A young woman in an animal-skin coat nurses a child,

the boy and girl beside her talk and laugh like spectators
at a Chinese soccer game. An older man spins something
like a large extravagantly decorated hat atop a broomstick,

colored rings and ribbons rising up, chiming, and relaxing
with each turn. Some men stamp out the fire and cross
to a large boulder where they undo two squarish bundles.

Two corpses roll out in fetal position, naked,
their gender and age unintelligible. Laying them out
on their bellies, the six men start their work. Sun

begins to show us color on the ridges of the mountains,
spreading, illuminating this rocky valley
where starting at the necks the corpses are skinned,

the sheets of skin tossed to the men behind,
who cut them into small squares;
the muscles are pulled from bone, limbs disjointed from body,

bones crushed in a white powder with a rock.
It is like a butcher shop. Pounding, hacking, slapping.
Hundreds of vultures wait on the rocks or circle

or—swooping down to the boulder too early—are shooed away
by the corpse-cutters. I cringe when they get to the feet,
and look back to my bicycle, which is delicate,

dark, pretty by the whitened river. By now sky is light,
the city awake: trucks and tractors rumble,
loudspeakers resume broadcasting political homilies.

I pass my waterbottle to friends. Some of us sit alone and stare.
Some of us hold each other. A few look through binoculars.
Everything is clicking, rhythmic:

chanting, the voices directing from the central government,
chopping, the river hissing, vultures gliding or preening,
small, reverent, nervous, or revolted gestures of tourists.

Supports and resistances move. At least for now and perhaps
for a while afterward I can discard my fears
or walk around them like furniture.

I will be dismembered, insensible, incomprehensible—
but, lucky accident, my flesh aches and lusts.
At last the corpse-cutter wraps the head in a cloth,

holds it up to the sky, prays, places it in a hollow,
and smashes it with a rock.
Two others cross to the flat where we stand

and drive us back a few steps. Bloody hands and bloody knives.
One of them taps me with his blade.
I check my sleeve for a stain, but I'm clean.

The ground here, frozen most of the year,
is no good for burial. There's too little timber for cremation.
The body means nothing when the soul is gone.

Sometimes the Tibetans leave their dead
in a river to be eaten by fish.
We say dust to dust. This is flesh to flesh.

Vultures, symbols of peace,
the carnivore self that does not kill,
circle huge, horrible, beautiful, black-white in the blue,

the white Vs of their bodies and their wingtips' feathers
spread my fingers against a sky the color
of the turquoise jewelry the Tibetans wear. The vultures eat.

I must get my visa at the Nepalese consulate.
As we ride back together Anna says, "I felt we were no better
than the vultures." "Really?" I say. I'm enjoying

the view of the Potala, people selling their wares,
my legs peddling, the clanking bike, the sun on my face.
I search for some guilt, but find nothing—

only this happiness, wind, elation, breath, circling.

Lhasa, Tibet

At a Truckstop in Gyantse, Tibet

It was the worst hotel yet and we were sharing a bed
in a room with seven other people.
I washed my hair at the cold water spigot in the parking lot.
Travelers sat on sunny steps outside their rooms,
smoking, or breakfasting on the last of their supplies.
The ruins of a fortress overlooked the truckstop.
On the opposite hill an earthen wall rippled
below the monastery's gold roofs, and the temple
with painted-on eyes looked back.

Around the dusty town's fleshy mud houses,
a green plain of barley fields
and mountains beyond.
Two boy-monks in silk orange robes and tennis shoes,
their heads shaved, faces dirty and smiling,
guided us through the temple to the roof
as we all spoke with our hands.
Everything opened in light up there.

After supper in a restaurant, our group walked back
to the truckstop, a little tipsy from the beer.
Magda in baggy black, a Croatian from Trieste, explained,
"I'm named for Magdalena, the greatest whore in history."
At the doors to our rooms she whispered to him,
"Spend the night with me and change your life."
When he told me, we laughed. It made it better for us.
We lay in the dirt behind the hotel. Dogs barked.

For a moment a woman shone her flashlight over us,
looking for a place to squat.
The moon and Milky Way's long cloud gleamed
from her hand, over the town
where we lived a few days—
the fortress, donkeys and corpulent mud houses,
young monks and seeing temple—
the universe condensed in an instant.

Sun Fields in Tibet

Sunrise in Tibet. Bright mustard fields
under ghostly mountains. Mud houses,
people working hunched over in the chill.
The bus bumps constantly

on the dirt road to Nepal, and I have to piss.
Exhaust comes in through the floor.
Open the window. We shiver to save our breath.
We cough in the dust.

Discomfort and joy.
Fire in the clouds. Merciless, lovely sky
above the barren grays and blues.
Muscular mountains.

Two donkeys and two horses graze.
A smiling boy waves
from the yellow field, the cold sun
on his shoulders, the mountains behind him black.

Blue Room, Blue Horse

Blue Room, Blue Horse

The doctors don't know why it hurts, so I ride
it out, as ordered, take pills, and ride
a galloping blue horse around the world's circumference,

through the starving hands in Somalia,
holding out their bowls. My head-weight clangs
against my collarbone and voices say it's hell

as the blue hooves clamor down broken halls
of Bosnian nursing homes while the dogs of the underworld
howl with the sirens howling their intent to help.

The flickering light hurts my eyes and the horse
won't stop. I can't listen to the authorities
debate solutions. It's mid-August, warm, still. Blue

curtains filter twilight onto white walls, blue.
Outside, trees are blue bouquets
lined up on the horizon.

When everything shadows blue, what was is not,
is a haze over fear yet is clear,
a blue, glazed bowl inside a blue bowl circling

inside my aching head. What is it?
Are physical ailments an echo of emotions
and a headache the price of doubt or fear

or suffering with those suffering on TV?
Or is it that blow to my head, months ago,
when I was hit, my packages lifted slowly by nothing

out of my arms, then the crack of my head on pavement,
and the membrane around my brain weakened
permanently, as they explain in science magazines,

which I can't read right now while the room
is turning blue. It is a sign from the body:
the impatient, hungry, blue horse galloping

pain into my head while the room turns bluer.
The names of the sky and the sea seem also to be
the beginning of darkness or the color of veins.

Prussian, ultramarine, cerulean, cobalt, cornflower,
and indigo unreadably shift on my hands as I write.
Through the clattering bowls comes the wild blue horse!

First Memory in Nova Scotia

In the morning I go to Yiayia's room.
She combs my hair, ties it, shows me
my reflection in the mirror: I am
a girl crowned with my blond curls.
When I look up from breakfast I see
Dad carrying Mom downstairs—both
smiling, especially Mom who's pregnant
and whose face I see full on. I'm almost
three. My brothers aren't born.

Dad loads wood into the stove.
Mom gives me a colander
for the blueberries I pick.
When we go to the beach, Yiayia and I
swim. Water's so cold Mom and Dad
watch from the shore. But held against
her fat body I don't feel cold. Waves
lift us slowly, put us down slowly.
The sky is the blue bowl where

our two heads float. On the way home
singing the alphabet, I think *elemenopi*
is a word like a deer leaping in woods
where the blueberries are. But then
orange flags across the windshield,
men signaling, and a deep hole in the road.
I cry out. We'll drop in, the car flip,
and our bodies fall. I don't know how
my happy word drove us to the edge.

Spirals

When I was a child I dreamt my mother died.
Afterward I couldn't watch television.
That wooden box where anything could happen

brought back the dream.
The Twilight Zone was especially awful,
the way a child could run away fast down

a dark street and still fall into another world.
Sometimes I amused myself with my mother's stockings,
a fur coat and handkerchiefs that were my grandmother's,

old cloisonné compacts and lipsticks, all family
treasures I'd found before, like the books I read
again and again, familiar yet surprising plots.

But always I forgot where not to look and found
the earrings lying in the pink plush of her jewelry box,
two black onyx tear drops surrounded by silver spirals

that made me sick to my stomach, like spinning around
too long looking at the sky, then falling down
with my gut spiraling into my eyes. It was *Vertigo*,

Jimmy Stewart at San Juan Bautista looking down
the tower stairwell that rushed toward him and away,
the curl spiraling at the back of Kim Novak's head

as she looked at the painting of the curl spiraling
at the back of a dead woman's head.
So in my dark closet and wrapped in blankets I sat

with my head against my knees, thinking the universe
had to end, but beyond any ending I could imagine
was more space, another universe. I couldn't stop

thinking about the universe which was so large
it blacked out the world. Here is my model
for everything I don't understand, for insomnia,

for my grandfather folding his coat, taking off his hat,
sailing from a rooftop to the asphalt of Colorado Springs,
for my uncle taking pills, having lunch with his daughter,

then lying down to die. Here are the far away lovers.
All of them. Here are two black tears surrounded
by silver spirals which I took from my mother's box

without asking—I knew she wouldn't mind. I would say
they bring me close to her. They don't. They are tokens
of my fear, beautiful and well-made. They could be

stupid postcards that say, "Wish you were here,"
and the earrings swing from my ears,
heavy silver and stone.

Street Names

I read all the street names as we drove to visit him,
wondering who named them, remembering older neighborhoods
in Bloomington, where quiet maples arch over brick streets.

I listed them—Hunter, Woodlawn, Atwater, Hawthorne, Park—
on my way home from school. And around every corner
of thought, the night we took Bill to the hospital.

The attendant brought the wheelchair and asked
where was the sick man. Bill said, *I'm not him*,
as we urged and eased him in.

There's no ease in the changed eyes of a man
with cancer in his brain. She said his thoughts
went one-two-one. No three. The mind was compressed,

helplessly enfolding malignant darkness.
He explained the picture wheel. Wheel is my word.
He drew the wheel in hospital air.

When the pictures went bad, he used to know to wait
and make them good again. Now he couldn't. He began to cry.
Daily he greeted my mother in a jacket and tie

and said, *It's time to go home.* Or he'd walk her
to the hospital parking lot and invite her to sneak away.
They were inevitably subject to betrayal.

Before we knew, we spent an afternoon on a friend's houseboat.
Bill watched Mom and me swim from boat to boat.
He made sexy jokes and giggled, comfortable in his chair.

We ate stir-fried chicken, drank no wine,
and watched the sun set over the lake. It was late May.
I took some photographs. Houseboat, houseboat.

The deck off the cabin was like a little porch. In Indiana
in late May we have crickets and fireflies in the fields.
I hung my head out the car window to feel the evening breeze

and see the lights. I read all the names of the streets,
just as today I list the familiar streets of Bloomington
and see them populated with no one I now love.

I dreamt the day we were told happened again.
Exhausted with weeping, she took a shower.
I watched her undress. She is over sixty

and has a beautiful body, my mother's body.
She said, *You and I belong to different worlds.
In my world people die.* It was only a dream,

but it was a cruel thing for a mother to say.
I couldn't cross over to where she was. I am her child
and as her daughter I am to be her child. One-two-one.

Spring Flick

Tonight you remember adolescence in Indiana
when on a dirty floor a girl laid out cards
and read your fortune.
Dogwood, forsythia, and redbud bloomed
in humid air, in the smell of cut grass.
Irises stems held up lanterns of desire.
The girl, the house, the verdict elude you.
All detail is forgotten, except
you remember that then, as now,
you wondered, how can spring remain outside me?
And you stood in the warm night
listening to the desolate sound of your own eyes
blinking in the dark.

The Black Room

Then the night was black black.
When I was in that room, I was in deep.
I could pass for eighteen in the bars
when I wore the right clothes.

A boy and I took sleeping bags to a field.
Red clay stuck in the grooves of our shoes.
It was wet around us and we each
put a hand in the other's jeans.

I wondered how to breathe,
and hung on to the edge.
Afterwards alone I pushed
right over it thinking about all the circles

our bodies made in the muddy field.
All this time I was thinking how
to live my life, how I would not
be like my parents, how I would.

With no one but a boy I knew
even then didn't matter much and no experience
of my own, I was trying to decide
how to make it happy.

Sometimes I couldn't stay in that room
though I'd painted it all black
with a few stars and moons. I liked it.
The summer leafy and light at the windows

and the walls' darkness wrinkled by that light.
I took my dog deep in the woods
or lay face down in the grass smelling
all the summers of my childhood in it,

making a jungle of the blades.
Or walked around town barefoot with nothing
but a dime for a phone call
in the change pocket of my jeans,

even if it were the middle of the night
and everything asleep but the crickets.
The drunks had shouted their last shouts,
leaving the bar. Whoever was going to make it

in a car had, and was looking out the window.
The moon and Venus chased each other
across the mountain ridges, danced a moment
with their reflections,

and the lake's chest breathed slowly.
Then the car's headlights
pushed uphill into the pine grove
and disappeared.

Whatever it was that forced me out I called
despair. I looked at my dirty bare feet
on the pavement and thought, I'm just going
from one black room inside to another outside.

I tried to picture whom to risk my dime on
to reach, relishing the desire—
as now I imagine why I wanted
to walk it off, wanted to walk away.

Days of 1976

Liz and I are old friends. Today hanging out
    we don't talk much. But it's nice
we are together in some yard across town
    when I hear "Unbroken Chain" for the first time:
a jet streaks; a high-pitched whir
    from speaker to speaker pulls me taut
like a white sheet across humid sky,
    and my muscles tighten at my skull
and at my ears while the day drones with cicadas
    during the open-windowed hot drive
to the lake and the hood quickly eats up highway lines.

We wake buzzing on rocks, flies creeping
    on our skin like eyelashes.
Swinging out on a rope daredevil I drop
    into the lake to loll, fetal position,
to hear the motorboats' heartbeat.
    Nightfall we find a new party somewhere
on the Colorado River. As always,
    guns at the hip and in the racks of pickups.
We dance and talk and eat potato chips
    while a man and a woman scream
at each other across the bonfire.

Meanwhile the Houston man who's on the lam,
    who ran down the backstairs
with his cocaine while the police ran up
    the front, turns me on
to coke and we fuck on the soft grass
    of the riverbank. Grinning and numb-gummed,
I feel neither lust nor shame.
    I find Liz and invite her for a swim.
We talk alone. I think for a second
    he was so stupid he could hardly talk.
Letting the thought slip away like my breath

or bubbles silently popping on the water's surface,
    I give in to air, to stars spreading
to inscrutable water and skin
    while my cool legs secretly kick.
Cocaine slides down the back of my throat
    and my jaw tightens; I feel it
beginning again, longing shaping something
    sad and exquisite in the water.
I remember and want to find it
    and to hear it again and again,
the song whose name I have not yet learned.

A Declining Neighborhood

If you pay attention to all the random events
in the news, if you imagine a map of the city,
plotting where everyone in an alley

with a knife is, and if you place yourself
in your small rooms, the front and back stairways
are prospects of violation and escape.

Everyone in a window is looking out and in,
not looking out for you,
only looking.

You pray you hide your thoughts
well enough to be legal and send your manuscripts
to several friends for safe keeping,

hoping they are friends still.
You blamed it on the goatee, sign of bad intent,
that he briefly wore—yet you can't forget

his eye burning orange despite tender gestures.
You closed your eyes to close out his, feeling guilty
for the betrayal, for making him a mere sensation.

You can't put together
why the surfaces are good and white
while cockroaches breed behind the walls,

why you are sorry he makes you miserable,
sorrier he makes you happy. You are sorry for him.
You watch him from the window as he goes to work.

A Doberman barks at him through his chainlink fence.
All day long the crackling as kids set off fireworks
and they set garbage on fire to make fire-engines scream.

That crazy guy next door clanging and clanging
before his garage full of junk is straightening out nails,
for Christ's sake. You sit inside listening to each one,

identifying your neighbors' thumpings on the stairs,
waiting for his steps, then the welcome snap of the deadbolt.
You can't wait for him to make you safe again.

Seen from my Window in San Francisco

Morning fog flattens the city.
   Alexander pesters two women,
      particularly the fatter one in a red sweater
who leans into the street
   to see if the bus is coming.
      Alexander jabs his index finger into air,
as if he were jabbing the flesh
   in her unbecoming sweater.
      He's probably saying, "Goddamn cocksucker!"
the way he always does, in rhythm,
   hard consonants too hard, 's' spit out
      so you can't forget the meaning.
Leaning into the street again,
   commiserating with her friend,
      she tries to ignore him.
But now she's lost her temper.
   She must be saying, "Leave us alone!"
      or "Go to Hell!"
and she shakes
   her plastic shopping bag for emphasis.
      She's spoken Alexander's language.
He stalks off toward Faye's Cleaners
   and comes back fresh with new material.
      Can't she tell he's crazy?
Of course, I don't like to talk to him either,
   though he's not all bile.
      One day in the laundromat he brought Nancy
(the one who yells, "Fuck the world!"
  at five in the morning)
     some cheese and crackers, because,
he said, "I'm your friend."
   And now she's sitting in a doorway
      watching him.

At last the bus arrives. The sun comes out,
   is new paint on the Victorians,
      restores them with shadow and volume.
Alexander watches the bus climb Eighteenth
   and mimes the driver steering,
      swaggering like Charlie Chaplin,
calling out to delivery trucks,
   buses, cars.
      He speaks gently to forlorn Nancy
while she finishes her coffee,
   gathers her wraps,
      walks away, saying nothing.
He stoops in the doorway and collects her garbage,
   crosses after her a few paces behind,
      his unshaven face contracting,
the pointed nose reaching almost to his underbite,
   the jaw working out words
      as the streetlight flashes from WAIT to WALK.

What's the Matter?

All our kitchen windows look out
on the airshaft. A woman
is putting things in a cardboard box.
Is she leaving?
A man in jeans and undershirt walks in.
He's smoking. A child goes to the box
and touches something.
The man pushes the object down.

He's got his hands on his hips
and walks toward the child who retreats
out of sight and reappears in the hall
around the corner. I guess he's been bad.
I know what it's like to be bad.
Sometimes you can't help it.
I'm sitting on the fire escape. What good
is a wooden fire escape? These questions

I can't help asking may have answers
that don't matter. What's the matter?
I want to go upstairs or outside
and down the street to another city
or even another house. So what
if there's so much to do?
I wish I could laugh at myself
but am complaining, which only keeps me here,

the sound of a football game on TV,
Sunday, the sun hot. This house standing
on a slope, the city stacking up-
ward and downward from it
as if it were in the middle of everything—
the mountains and the sea,
sidewalks, the sky, the sigh
of traffic—all pressing against its walls.

This is not the house, but me.
The window above the packing family
is open. A man in white is smoking,
facing a woman who washes dishes and talks
about making chicken. Downstairs
the child is alone in the kitchen
opening up Tupperware containers.
His mother gives him more and

he opens them and seems content.
The man in the undershirt
is scratching his head, looking down
at the child. He and the woman squat,
the child between them. They wrap
dishes in newspaper, stack them in a bucket.
Family harmony at last. But upstairs
the man in white yells, "She's Greek!"

I'm Greek. What's wrong with that?
The white curtain is half-blown
outside the window, puffed up
like a pair of Victorian bloomers.
The woman washes dishes.
"I told him I felt discouraged," she says.
"I hate dirt."
So do I.

I look at the sky.
It's Indian summer in San Francisco.
The weather is perfect.
Her eyes meet mine across the airshaft.
She says, "There's no place I can go."
And so my neighbor reveals what—
when you asked, "What's the matter?"
and I answered, "I don't know"—
I wished I could say, but could not.

Sadness

Rilke says sadness is the moment the future enters us
by surprise and pushes us into the unknown.
The handsome bartender says, "Your drinks are on me"
—and leans across the counter—"What'll it be?"

Alcohol is heat in my ears as I catch my reflection
in the mirror, happy flirting without forethought.
But days later alone the question comes back:
What *will* it be?

and I remember moments with you
when time raced quickly around us like a romping young dog
and we were amused. Today time reminds me of the hound
knowingly guarding the underworld. Sadness slips in,

doesn't it? even in the gentle pleasures of the body
which pass too and remind us of loss.
Rilke says be attentive and patient with sadness
because it is our way of learning through solitude.

In your eyes I see your solitude watching mine.
I note the line in your cheek when you smile.
Our sad fate enters me. When we are sad together
or sad apart, how attentive and patient will we be?

The Dog

I take the dog to the beach
and people smile at me like children,
the way people smile
at the parents of infants.

He is innocent, and seeing him
they too feel innocent for a moment.
The drunk woman sitting with her boyfriend
calls out, "Is that your puppy?"

"No, he's a friend's puppy,"
I call back, smiling. And I think,
actually, I'm his goddamn stepmother.
I walk far down the beach. I have to.

I fell in love with a man
who's got joint custody of a dog.
It's cold and foggy. I walk hard
and look at footprints instead of the ocean.

He's the embodiment of past love,
gets the pure affection,
pushes me to the edge of the bed,
persists in licking us when we make love.

"What kind of dog is that?" a man asks.
"Yellow lab."
"Sure seems to be having a good time."
He's beautiful, running, his legs flying out,

so he seems suspended over the sand
which is kindred,
though he's slightly blonder.
I collect sand dollars and he's interested,

dark eyes and golden face smiling.
He chases gulls and pipers, confronts
all other dogs, and circles back to me
for confirmation or reproval.

When we get in the car he sits
in the passenger seat, surveys a while,
then lays his head on my lap,
and I stroke it, just like a lover.

Jack's Defeat Creek

My old flame lives by Jack's Defeat Creek
where the privets are in flower, fragrant,
    abundant with bees; three children tumble
in the yard; and a group of friends
cooks outside, grabbing their bellies,

laughing about how much they have to lose.
My old friend lives by Jack's Defeat Creek.
    He and his wife don't touch.
Their son pinches the heads of flowers
because, I'm angry, he says.

If I saw them kiss it might be worse.
This is the house that Jack built
    where I swing on the porch,
the guest the children sit beside.
My friends laugh, "No more hot peppers!"

Oh, we still have our appetites,
but can't stand the consequences.
    My old flame takes my hand.
We're here to do the work of love, he says,
and what is raising children but the work

of love? I say I like being
alone, but mean I want to be alone
    with someone on that first hill of passion
when we were all confused, when Jack
fell down and broke his crown

and Jill came tumbling after, overcome,
like him. Oh, but who is Jack?
    Who fell in the creek in dire defeat
and was it by woe or war?
It's Jack in Jack's Defeat Creek.

On the Hottest San Francisco Day in Recorded History, He Plays Piano and She Listens

She recognizes the music her grandmother used to play.
Once, when the girl took lessons,
her grandmother played a piece by Mozart
that the child had stumbled through
not understanding its potential.

The grandmother played so beautifully
the girl leaned her head against the piano
and sobbed as if for inevitable disappointment.

It is quiet and hot all around the music.
How light-headed she feels—dry heat pushing her
into some clear, unexpected blue place

where newspapers identify currents of the soul:
record heats that will be superseded by new ones,
surprise aftershocks of the quake that was not the big one.

She can hear her grandmother saying,
"One thing in my life I'm happy about—
I fell in love only once."

Though as a child she learned to doubt her grandmother
who told fictions, sometimes to awe her
and sometimes to frighten her into good behavior,

the woman believes her, that she fell in love only once,
that when the handsome captain
first came to her family's home in Constantinople,

her grandmother arrived finally
and fully in her heart. Though he has been dead
longer than they were married, she still calls out,
"Vassili!" in her sleep. The woman listening

remembers a dream—in the transport of lovemaking
she asked, "Why can't it be like this forever?"
and her lover replied, "If it were forever,
it wouldn't be *this*." She knows she is

all the characters in her dream.
She can't find a place for her heart to stay;
she can't find a place in her heart to stay.

She watches the man's back as he plays,
the child's pain written on his back,
the movements of his fingers noted on his back—
and his arms are like wings, she thinks.

She cannot think what the music is like,
only that, light in the heat, happy and sad,
it rests nowhere as if it could be like this forever.

BLUE EARTH

Blue Earth

The moving van slowed uphill under my possessions:
jewels, lifework, junkboxes.
The turtle with the world on its back.

Mile markers rushed by.
The truck crossed the Missouri River into the Midwest,
and I left California's promise.

Just when I thought, "There will be no more,"
I saw a sign, BLUE EARTH. A town perhaps
named over a century ago

by someone who could see the earth from space,
a Winnebago holy man who prophesied
the moonshot photograph.

Then I guess the land was stolen by settlers
who counted blessings in corn flourishing lush
blue in the haze and summer storms.

Affliction was the twister that ripped away a wall
but left the Afghan hanging on the rocker-back,
every dish in the hutch intact.

And then snow came,
the sky cleared,
and the fields turned blue again.

I imagine the faithful filing into church
to kneel and clasp their hands in the awkward pews,
then to bear witness to the commonplace in the graveyard.

I don't know how they broke the frozen earth for the dead.
Now I see my old life everywhere it isn't. Here
the lakes tell me brightly how the light looks:

the *now* in all the *ohs* the sun reflects on water—
then my awe becomes a history,
open-ended as loss, and I need

to make it like something I see:
white barnsides in the morning
next to rectangular black fields just like billboards

advertising WHITE and BLACK
or the real billboard exhorting, PRAY! IT WORKS!
as I drive to work.

My soul under winter, my sad sleep
are like black dirt
and corn stubble,

or the white farmhouse and the white barn
lit up unlikely, like *hope* or *home*,
the white house and the white barn followed

by another house and barn that almost seem to yearn.
Just when I thought "There will be no more," I saw
Blue Earth. Hope, harvest, stubble, title of my days.

In the New Year

I take my dog across the frozen lake.
Some days the snow and ice make light.
Not so today.

Under white sky the white lake
doesn't shine, but stretches out to a bank
of spiky black trees.

In places ice rises up
like waves. Thin sheets break through
as if in an instant

the cold had stilled a storm.
And it is quiet
except for the shush

of my boots flattening snow
and a heaving and scraping like a huge clock.
I imagine under my feet

an iceman labors,
turns the sprockets to keep the machine
moving, the work of winter, the neighbors

shoveling under the wheels of their cars.
And me, I shovel, too—clockwork.
The dog fetches the ball.

I throw, watch him running ahead.
I bend, throw again, walk on
into the nullifying white.

Though in this season the lake is frozen
so deep they drive trucks across,
they say you hear the ice shifting.

My dog too hears the sound
and stands a moment,
head cocked, ears forward and alert.

Then he leaps, races, digs beneath
the crests of frozen waves, and turns to me
his snowy snout grinning.

Nothing else moves.
The city and its capitol, my home
among other houses and yards

line the shore like relics.

Winter and War on Lake Monona

I call my dear friend Edwin Honig
because winter is a burden to me.
It is like an ice block on each shoulder,
all the muscles tightening around my heart.

He says his college days in Madison
almost took his manhood. We laugh.
And he advises I buy a few pink
light bulbs to shed warm light around me

and start a story about our phone call
in which the student who read a newspaper
in my class is the same one I discover
fishing in an ice hut on Lake Monona.

Then I will have started a splendid event.
Indeed, who is this boy-man
who follows world affairs in spite of me
and my books? He sits alone

on the ice with a bottle of vodka
and he reads that yesterday the Iraqis
bombed Tel Aviv, the coalition forces
destroyed a hydro-electric plant

and a factory that, depending on who's
reporting, manufactures baby formula
or biological weapons. It is so cold
we must breathe through our scarves

and our eyes tear. I think how tough he is,
patiently drinking as he guards the hole
in the ice, as his father and uncles did.
Every few minutes we hear warnings

on the weather channel: prolonged exposure
to cold can lead to irrational thinking
and death. Yet here he does for sport
what before was done for survival,

as if one could be impervious to the elements.
"Good boy, good boy, good boy,"
my student says as he bends to pet my dog.
What will this man do? He shows me pictures

of tortured POWs. I show him the box
of pink light bulbs I've bought.
Then we stand together a little embarrassed,
the tears freezing on our cheeks.

I carry home my fragile load,
and when I turn on the lights
—oh, splendid event!—
the white walls are warm like flesh.

More Than a Month of Gray Winter in Madison

No one says, "What a beautiful day!
The sky is so gray!"
So why should I feel bad for feeling bad
when the whole city is pale

as if God had stretched out a cold wet rag,
then clamped it down with his enormous thumb.
And would it be easier if I believed in a god,
as the early settlers did? They understood

gratitude. The soil here is good, supremely good.
He ordered the seasons: the black earth rests
in winter, delivers its reward in summer.
And it is good to separate good from evil,

the now from the future, to know the virtue
of suffering without despair,
though newspaper articles and the stiff photographs
from the 1890s depict madness and suicide:

children lying before the family hearth, side by side
in caskets; the woman in the swamp,
grinning wide, her arms arched above her head,
snakes tight in her grasp.

She held their vileness high for the lens to record.
Today the local comic-strips joke
about our collective north winter blues.
Windows iced-over and dim

make sense of the saying, darkness closes in.
The sun sinks at four and we're Mad City,
not the Madison named for the luminary democrat.
Atop the capitol the gold goddess of progress

almost gleams, already frozen in the gray sky
while below her a roller-blader glides
beside the not-yet-frozen lake.
He moves fast but his lunges are slow,

graceful, easy, propelled by powerful muscles
and something in his dogged, forward posture.
From the sidewalk I'll soar into spring,
I guess, on still icy silver wings.

Dream with Billie Holiday

In dreams East is West.
                        I squat beside a tide pool,
feeling the anemone close around my finger. Cliff-spray flies
with the gulls and I'm with a lover I haven't seen in
decades. That first night,
                           hearing her
voice
in the dark room as if hands stroked my whole body
and the dark were night waves,
I was quiet but overcome by something like what holds
waves up a moment
so high before the boom and sibilance.
"Who's this?" I asked. "Billie Holiday," he said.

Now it's much the same;
his body still wiry, his hair still black,
he bends bare-chested over his guitar.
                              I only see
the years intervene in the expression on his face.
At last I say, "We weren't so nice to each other."
"I've heard that complaint before," he answers, a bit resigned.
"I meant me," I say, "I wasn't so nice."
                                Then to punctuate
the half-lie I press my palms into the small of his back.
And I hear waves breaking in my hair, in the pillow,

and in our illicit kiss.
Back then we kissed and told,
                        so all our kisses were new.
When he slept with a dental hygienist who slept with the
dentist, he smiled ironically, playing his thin fingers
across my hip as if it were his guitar.
                                I saw a swan
floating in each of his teeth and wondered
                                    why the god
transformed himself into a gaudy stupid bird,

                                        why his eyes were green
as the new leaves outside the window
Even as I wanted him all the more,
                        the swan
provoked a memory of his bragging. He read only the old poets
and thought all the new bad. So
                        I was bad. One morning
I came to him. I kissed his neck
                        and he kissed mine and
found an illegible haiku there. "Tell," he said.
"No." "Tell," he pleaded. "No," I laughed.

Years later in a place we never were,
we are as wild as we were that morning. I hear
sea lions moan from the boulders and piers
                        and the room is loud
with ocean and the moon-face fills the window
with an open-mouthed sigh.
Then I see Billie Holiday standing in the door,
mock-shocked, laughing behind her hand, singing,
   I've been seen with someone new,
   But does that mean I'm untrue?
                        Then I'm back,
standing beneath frozen by sunny buds. I've stopped
myself. It is the January thaw in Wisconsin—
        the sunlight tricking me
into remembering something—that begins this dream.

Walking to Work in Milwaukee

I can't tell if the forecast is golden or dire.
The weather turns from cold to bitter.
My career is uncertain and the wind is splinters

in my cheeks. I scowl at crosses, Jesuit banners
honoring good works, the stars and stripes
atop every tall building, and I smile

at the red-cheeked woman running for the bus.
At her feet are litter and ice; on the trashcan
a sign reminds us every litter-bit hurts.

The weather turns from cold to bitter.
Do the thinly dressed sit in the cathedral
for solace or warmth? Where do they go

to sleep? I know I'm entitled to nothing
yet my undemocratic heart disagrees.
I can't tell if the forecast is golden or dire.

First the scene where they dangle bread
before the hungry. Then the other
where they lay dozens of roses in my arms

and applaud loud and long, the scene before
I wake and ask, Who are the *they*?
My career is uncertain and the wind is splinters.

They are incoherent. They are not complacent.
They are tired. Some are angry, some greedy,
some cruel. They want, bless, confess. I can't read

the immense countenance of streets or sky.
I can't tell if the forecast is golden or dire.
The sky is clear, dry, blue, cold;

the streets, dirty and interesting.
At the mission, people smoke, indifferent,
lean an elbow on an outspread knee.

A sign reads, Jesus saves. One of many.
It's easy to be friends and easy to be afraid.
More difficult is pity and self-pity.

My career is uncertain and the wind is splinters,
In the elevator I stand, suspect among co-workers,
smelling their sick breaths as *good morning*

dully echoes *good morning, good morning,*
my keys in my coat pocket.
I can't tell if the forecast is golden or dire.

Green Shoes

Because it's mid-March
and most of the snow has melted,
you put on green shoes.
instead of boots.
You go down the steps too happy,
not noticing the night made ice.

For a wild instant you're in air,
then you crash, stairs jabbing your spine.
All winter comes back
in your pain and in what follows:
the petty with the profound,
the woman who snubs you on the bus,

your curses at fifteen below
when the car won't start, the war,
the daily grief in newspapers,
the prisoner fearful of footsteps,
rubbing feeling back
into cold hands and feet.

The dictator lines up his band.
Tenderly holding their black instruments
and kneeling, they play a funeral march
as they're shot.
You hear the crazy music from above.
You're making love.

They're throwing the dead
from the windows.
You think, We're helplessly
walking on air—
the lucky stay awhile.
Then you see green shoes

and a woman appears out of the dark,
as if she were opening a prison door,
and she helps you up from the stairs
and helps you to your feet.
She touches your bruised arm
and asks, "Are you sure you're all right?"

The Irises of the Midwest

In winter, sun is a crab burning
through black tree lace as the strict god
of country churches breathes in a headful
of ice. Snowy restraint. Yet spring's
a stain of iris beds that can't
be washed from the linens. Then sky
shrinks into a malevolent
blue eye while sinful petals bloom.

Rowing on Lake Mendota

The plump at the catch. The common exhalation.
The pull, feather, and glide. The timing. The trust
to speed backwards, to row in unison, each a mirror
of each squared oar pushing against the water again
and again, to be one boat in the amphitheater

of the nearby shore where the last light of sunset
is pink sinking over deep trees. Muscular memory.
The pause when the coxswain calls "Weigh enough!"
Four balancing oars. We float together and overhead
ducks stream from the crescent moon.

The Ferry to Serifos

Cavafy in the Early Morning

He can't look at the morning sea without seeing a boy,
perhaps the one in the café, making coffee,
watching it boil and foam three times.

In the monotony of dishes and voices,
old men rolling dice at backgammon,
the stench and haze of smoky air,

the young man's face
shines clearly,
etched by love.

He doesn't know fifty years after his death
his country will print his face on a postage stamp,
and below the face, *Greek Democracy*.

He stands looking long at the flat sunny sea,
the fishing boats toying with their lines.
The shore is empty, the water all-lighted, lovely,

the sky so blue and young he sees it
with a tint of pink flesh. Somewhere in dreams,
they still lie waking, limb across limb,

sweaty on summer sheets.
His illicit secret burns on his shoulder,
a tooth-mark rose.

The Cypress Trees of Mount Pelion

Through the cypresses' dark wings
was the city of Volos,
the midnight bay and white ferries.
I feared the high edge,
the fixed lights of houses falling under the mountain
as the old taxi floated around the curves.
We climbed,
wings appeared and reappeared
almost singing out,
as if asking to be the last beautiful thing.

Greek Easter

All the Greeks in Bloomington come here,
to Peter Costas's for Easter. Whole garbage cans
of roasted lamb
beside long tables of food, and ingredients—feta, filo,
olives—ordered from faraway Chicago.

We say, "*Kalo Pascha.*"

Vassili pinches both my cheeks and says, "*Koritsáki mou.*"
We click our eggs together
and the holder of the unbroken egg gets luck.
I ask my mother, "Why are all the eggs for Greek Easter red?"
"The red is the red of Christ's blood
and of the lamb's blood." "That's sad."
"Yes," she answers "but the eggs are for new life."

She doesn't say Christ died for our sins,
she never will,
though the neighborhood kids say my whole family
will go to hell for not going to church on Sundays.

To me, equal to Christ's story is the story of "that Helen,"
who was beautiful,
who ran away to Troy in spite of marriage and kin.
The sorrows, the strategies, the triumphs of the gods—
each is a red egg
piled high in a bowl.

I walk under the grape arbor, which is still in winter.
At dusk dancing begins.
My father leaps and turns in the air, arms spread
like island windmill sails. Then he holds the handkerchief
for my mother to lead, quick-footed and laughing.

My parents are beautiful. I wonder if they love each other,
though I'm sure they do, I'm not sure I believe what I see—

I go inside and sit with Doctor Frank.
His voice is calming, deep and slow. Then I go
outside and see smoke and a small fire
backlighting the corner of the yard
where my brothers and some other boys
compete to pee the highest, broadest arc.
I look at my white shoes. I can smell the delicious lamb.

Brothers

One brother sleep-walked in the garden,
looking for father. The other dreamed the dragon
fire-red with seven horns and ten heads.

But now my parents were together again
and we five traveled from the Greek mainland
to island and island, temple and church.

Many people on Patmos were cross-eyed
as if their vision were cursed by revelation.
A woman showed us the Cave of the Apocalypse,

the two hollows in the stone wall, silver-haloed,
where John laid his head and his hand, dreamed
shared suffering and kingdom and endurance.

She owned the only restaurant open
that time of year, took a liking to me, fed me
potatoes, onions, and eggs fried in olive oil,

then sat across the table, talking as I ate.
I was neither child nor adolescent.
She saw the child in a way that comforted me

and made me sad to say goodbye.
Winter and stormy—we left on a fishing boat,
the horizon lost to waves. Again and again,

the bucket with a line tied to its handle
was tossed puke-filled into the sea,
then retrieved, scoured by turbulence.

When I retell the story to my brothers,
I say I left the cabin's smelly misery
and lay in the life-raft, cool air an elixir,

my stomach pleasantly full. I was the only one
not sick and for the first time saw dolphins
rise up like waves out of the waves.

Funny how both my brothers also remember
the life-raft, dolphins, and being the only one not sick,
as if one could not suffer the others' suffering.

The Ferry to Serifos

The horizon slides up and down as the ship rocks
on mild summer waters. Slightly sickening.
Relentless memory and worry. As if there were a crack
in my brain like this wake churning white
in the sea's restful darkness. I doze and wake,
doze and wake. Can't tell whether it's dark
or light that agitates me. Gulls follow.
Above, luminous edges of pumping wings.
Below, they glide along the water's surface,
mimicking the dark fluttering in small waves,
swooping across the horizon like a song,
like a sustained voice, rising, falling.

At last I see Serifos, lovely beyond memory.
Ancient terraces, relics of cultivation,
meticulously lace the hillsides and hold narrow fields
of light. Rust of iron ore, gray-green rocks,
purple blooming thyme, olive and ochre grasses:
all complex but modest colors of the land
responding to the sea's vivacious blue.
The village is a white crown.
My house is up there, in need of a whitewash.
Blue windows and blue door. Cool tile floor.
I'll climb the village stairs and swim in the sea.
Health. Clarity. Hope. Everything like the blue light
of sea and sky augmenting each other,
the somber rocks and ebullient daisies.
Red poppies. A warmth calms my temples
as I lean on the rail, looking. Then shouts
of sailors handling line, anchors and chains clanking.
I gather my bags, stand with the others, and wait to land.

Anemos

       I don't want to hear the wind tonight
when blood on my thighs is relief
and sadness that there will be no child;
when wind moans as my abdomen aches persistently,
waking me from dreams I'd rather not face.
                                    Everyone
on this island knows the wind carries the voices
of ghosts. So I wish for comfort,
to interlace my limbs with a lovers',
for that sweetness. But the wind is not easy,
it's exacting.
                   It makes the shopkeepers irritable—
Anemos, polí ánemos they mutter, handing me my change.
The old men in the *kafenéion* roll their dice
with particular and vicious fervor.
                              I imagine
your hand, but the wind keeps asking
Whose hand? Which lover from which dream?

Today the children play soccer
in the marble square, chanting *Exo! Exo!*
when the ball is kicked out of bounds.
Now I chase the ball; now I've lost it.
Thrust out into the village maze,
I amble alone
               between white moonlit houses,
body hunched, jacket ballooning out behind me,
my face smoothed coolly by the wind's hand.

A Windy Night of Terror on Serifos

Spiros says vampires come out when the wind blows.
I don't believe that. Nor am I afraid of people
(though the wind's semblance of a person disturbs me).

I'm naked and alone in my bed, stiff with terror.
What if the door flies open? What would come in?
The streetlight reflecting on the marble of the piazza?

The wind hisses over the roof, knocks a tin can
around the square, shuffles grimy footsteps,
pushes the door open a crack, slams it closed.

Who's calling, trying to come in? The wind
and a thing inside me, flying against the walls
and threatening to get out, wildly.

Counting Time on Kímolos

Two months ago his brother wrote
   "I want the simplest of funerals"
      and swallowed a bottle of pills.
Now my father and I arrive at the decaying port
    where the small ship and the cement slab dock
       dominate a café,
a few flaking whitewashed houses,
   and a rocky quarter-moon beach.
      Eight tourists on the whole island.
Old women drive donkeys overwhelmed by wheat.
    An ancient urn still balances on a solitary pillar.
       The slats of shutters hang unpainted and askew.

This is not a happy island like Sifnos
   known for its excellent cuisine,
      its garbanzo bean soup
and a salad
   of fresh white *mizíthra*
      sprinkled on a rose of tomatoes.
There the port is lighted
   with strings of bare bulbs
      and the waiters bring carafes of local wine
to full seaside tables.
    Here it's a forty-five minute wait
      for an unsavory *souvlaki*.

But we are told, Go to the *panayiri*.
   In celebration of school's end
      teenagers do local and ancient dances
led by their elegant teacher,
   and his precise
      and passionate feet.
Relatives eat at windy tables.
    Children run in and out of the winding maze
      or climb on stage and repeatedly jump off,
untiring and unscolded.

>   Watchers join in the dance,
>   motivated by no apparent cue.

My father jokes that he too is part-Greek:
    "I'm related to Greeks by blood,
        after all, my children are Greeks."
Forty years ago against the wishes of families,
    my parents married and lived on the islands.
        My father learned the captain's dance,
to spin as he leapt high slapping his feet,
    then nearly falling,
        to recover
at the crucial second
    Opa! people cried,
        and threw plates to the floor.

Manos Hadzidakis, he remembers, told him
    Western music comes to a climax and ends,
        while Eastern music goes on,
sustained passion...some people get up to dance,
    others sit down, and the dance continues
        as my father takes my arm. We walk back
to the hotel in dim light. Ghosts of whitewash
    float up from darkened houses
        and white calla lilies float
above the simple pine box.
    Behind us is a celebration, music sustained,
        and dance—*Opa!*—whose end we will not see.

Portokali

The night before we went to Epidaurus
we stayed in a seaside town called Portokali.
Portokali means orange, both the fruit and the color,

as in English. We checked into "Mike's."
We were lucky to find a hotel in the off-season
and Mihali welcomed us.

From the balcony of our room we watched the sun set,
fishing boats slicing like small black knives
into the movement of light across the harbor,

the blinking of the lighthouse
becoming more intense as we drank thick Peloponnesian wine
we'd bought at a roadside stand where bottles,

bright in the sun, were arranged yellow, red, yellow, red.
All day round green hills of orchards,
trees forming smaller hills, round upon round,

dotted with oranges, happy color,
under the always too-blue-to-believe Greek sky.
That night we walked along flagstone streets

away from the houses to where there were no lights,
only the moon and a strong smell of oranges
rotting on the ground and on the side of the road,

our hands sticky from the ones
you pulled from a branch above our heads.
Looking back to Portokali and its lighthouse,

we paused where the graveyard was alive with light,
for in the village of the dead every tomb burns
with an oil lamp and an icon or two behind its window.

Who cares for them? Who strikes the match?
An old devout lady in black remembering sunny oranges
and our kiss as we walked back?

A Night in Rome

It was a day of brides.
This morning in the hilltop town of Orvieto
was a wedding we didn't see—just rice

on cobblestones and people lingering—
and one we did see in the grand cathedral
with its black and white marble stripes,

gold inlay and godly heights, the story
of Christ and his angels flying in frescoes
about her and the groom (whose too long trousers

pooled at his ankles). "Look, oh, look!"
we said on the night bus to the city.
There was the Colosseum lit up and a grassy hill

where hand-in-hand running, climbing,
shimmering in the headlights,
were the bride, lifting her skirts, and the groom.

Our hotel is near the train station
in the old red light district of Rome.
Five flights up with suitcases.

We've eaten prosciutto, asiago, and walnut bread.
Hot green olives washed down with Chianti
from a six hundred year old cellar in Tuscany.

Everything good to eat and good to say.
You lie on the bed; I stand
at the window and report:

a woman's taking off her clothes;
with her back to me she smiles
at her reflection.

No, it's a man, not a mirror,
and he's smiling at her.
Now you stand by me and spy.

Now we lie down and darken the room.
All the various warmths of making love,
(everything kisses).

Coming and crying,
as if it were new. *As if it were new*,
we think, and not now

and we were not returning to a place we know.
In the dark I listen to strange music.
The percussion of your heartbeat

and your breath, the little gusts on my forehead,
someone in the hall rattles a key, a drama on TV,
traffic, the two-pitched emergency sirens,

something I can't identify echoing in the airshaft.
Not a wind or a voice.
Not the lover's words sighing,

Angel and *Darling*. Not me
praying for your safety and perpetual return.
Under my ear, your chest rises and sinks and rises.

How fragile! I think, not believing it.
Everything passing like the repetition of
I love you. "Strange sounds," you say,

just as I thought you'd dozed off.
In a room that's held many passions,
we marry again.

And we're talking, showering, dressing,
locking the room, passing
the Colosseum, walking for hours in Rome.

The Bell

Sunday morning the bell calls
the people to worship.
Then the priest, who is so stiff
with sickness and age

that he can hardly rise
from his bench outside
the tiny theological library,
sings the mass like a young boy.

His voice makes those of us
still in bed soar like kestrels
piloting the wind
between rocky peaks.

But when the bell rings
at odd times
it means someone on the island
has died.

Then the old women congregate
outside the church gate and we hear
their voices questioning, "Who?"
until the name is spoken.

Today it was Maki. I heard
Kiría Mariniá's Parkinson-disease voice
utter an "Ahhh…"
descending and tripping,

a sonic representation
of an old woman's fear
that the force of the Meltemi wind
could fling her down

the very stone stairs
which are the streets,
and daily necessity demands
she climb them on arthritic legs.

This morning when the bell woke me,
you slept. I was glad
you were spared
one reawakening of grief.

The night before
the wind's urgent sound
you took to be
the storytelling of the dead.

You couldn't understand,
and it kept you sad, haunted,
thinking of the stories
your father's death deprived you of.

You sleep and I run my hand
over your back. Muscles strong,
skin freckled and warm—
signs of health from the sea.

The marble paved square
and whitewashed walls,
work of centuries, mirror heat,
and the wind drones on.

The priest sits,
blue and black robes fluttering
around his thinness.
When he says, "How are you?"

we respond in kind,
And he says, "Glory to God."
"Glory to God" for he lives,
though in a prison of pain,

and his belief makes death
the moment the spirit
wings out, invisible
above the stone walls of the village.

Pleasure Attained Morbidly, Harmfully

In Greek "kamaki" means harpoon. It also refers
to the young men who sit down with women in cafés
and press them with invitations
or sigh, "Sssss," or "Mounaki mou," my little cunt.
Yiannis, a notorious kamaki, a real fisherman,
takes women out in his boat, watches as they swim.
Later, at his sister's restaurant, he keeps
their wine glasses never empty and never full,
feeds them morsels from his catch. Today he sits with me,
"You're a woman who likes to be alone.
You go to the beach alone, you listen to your music alone,
and now you're going to your house to be alone.
Why don't you stay here?" He wants me to stay in the port,
where the discos and bars are,
but wherever we are, he says, there is a party.
The bus comes. "You're a strange woman," he says.
I ride up the mountain thinking I am strange.
I ask the priest sitting in the square how he is.
"Old and sick, my child." And he blesses me,
"Doxa to Theó." And asks after my grandmother and mother,
my father and brothers; he sends them greetings
and blesses them and blesses me again.
He doesn't know what I will do after I shut the door.

As my bathwater boils I read Cavafy.
He records that Imenos admonishes us "to love even more
pleasure attained morbidly, harmfully;
the body rarely feels what pleasure wants."

I pour hot water on myself, freeing my skin
from the salty tightness of the sea—
but the sun still burns in me,
soft and clean, alert with longing.
A stranger can kiss your neck and make you all cunt,
but that's not what pleasure requires,
it's not attained morbidly, harmfully enough.

That stupid man, with his table full of laughing
and flushed women, telling me who I am
as if his words could keep me speared and writhing.
He has an instinct for mere violation.
I could spit with scorn, like the priest's mad daughter.
But what is it? Is it Cavafy's despair?
"He's lost him completely. And now he tries to find
his lips in the lips of each new lover."
Is it going back and back to some imagined first place?
there where talking, gentle and gentled,
the body understood that *ekstasis*
is a being put out of its place.

On The Ship

This small one certainly looks like him,
this portrait drawn in pencil.

Quickly done, on the ship's deck;
a magic afternoon.
All around us, the Ionian Sea.

It looks like him. Only I remember him more beautiful.
He was sensitive until suffering,
and this lighted his expression.
More beautiful he appears to me,
now when my soul recalls him, out of Time.

Out of Time. All these things are so old—
the sketch and the ship and the afternoon.

Translated from the Modern Greek of C.P. Cavafy

Go to the Good and Return With the Good

> *You won't meet the Laistrygonians*
> *and the Cyclops and wild Poseidon,*
> *if you don't bear them along in your soul,*
> *if your soul doesn't raise them before you.*
> —C. P. Cavafy

When I left Serifos an hour ago,
    Kiría Mariniá stood in Halídas's store,
her jaw shaking, and said slowly,
    Go to the good and return with the good.
On the islands, more than in Athens and other cities,
    people keep their greetings and farewells:
blessings and good wishes for every time of day
    and year, for health, a trip, appetite,
a swim, and the long life of children.
    Go to the bakery or across the ocean,
and they say, *Sto Kaló*. To the good.

It's good to remember that those who say
    the islands are isolated are mistaken.
Islands aren't self-sufficient and never were.
    The old men sit all afternoon in the *kafenéion*
playing gin rummy and backgammon,
    smoking, drinking Greek coffee or ouzo,
and eating *mezedes*—small plates of cucumber,
    olives, feta, and cubes of bread
topped with sardines, all stuck with toothpicks.
    Everything savored slowly, slowly.
Sigá, Sigá. They can always tell you
    when the boats come and from where.

At each docking a crowd gathers to see
    who's returned, with whom, and how many tourists.
In the ancient commerce between the islands
    friends and family depart and arrive,
to go to Athens or to fish. Lovers separate

and in the journey there might be another.
There's always the possibility of return.

At the ferry's stern I watch goodbye a long time.
    Look back, look back to the night village—
window lights gathered at the mountain summit
    and the lighthouse rhythmically
rolling its Cyclops eye, recalling that on Serifos
    Odysseus blinded the one-eyed monster,
whose dark head might float below
    the agitated wake. On my tongue is
tangy sea air—*wanderlust, luxury, tender, commerce.*
    Will the words ferry me to the other side?
Go to the good and return with the good?
    Lights of other shores, other
ships rise from the horizon, and I sail on,
    look back until the island
then the lighthouse disappear, loved.

Notes

Epigraph
I translated the lines by Cavafy throughout the book.

❦

"First Memory in Nova Scotia" (p. 25)
Yiayia — Grandmother.

❦

"Cavafy in the Early Morning" (p. 67)
Constantine Cavafy (1863-1933) was a Greek poet from Alexandria.

❦

"Greek Easter" (p. 69)
Kalo Pascha — Happy Easter.
Koritsáki mou — My little girl (literally my little daughter), a common term of endearment.

❦

"The Ferry to Serifos" (p. 73)
Serifos is an island in the Cyclades in Greece.

❦

"Anemos" (p. 74)
Anemos — Wind.
Kafenéion — Café.
Anemos, polí ánemos — Wind, a lot of wind.
Exo! Exo! — Out! Out!

❦

"A Windy Night of Terror on Serifos" (p. 75)
Piazza is a Greek loan-word from Italian.

☙

"Counting Time on Kímolos" (p. 76)
Kímolos and Sifnos are islands in the Cyclades in Greece.
Mizíthra — Goat cheese that is softer, less salty, sweeter than feta.
Souvlaki — Shish-ka-bob.
Panayiri — Festival, from paneyiris, meaning all come together.
Manos Hadzidakis is a well-known Greek composer and songwriter.

☙

"Portokali" (p. 78)
In Greece the tombs are often built with small recessed altars behind a glass door. Inside are candles, oil-lamps, ikons, and other religious objects.

☙

"The Bell" (p. 83)
Meltemi — A strong wind from the South that blows for days at a time.

☙

"Pleasure Attained Morbidly, Harmfully" (p. 86)
Doxa to Theó — Glory to God.

☙

"Go to the Good and Return with the Good" (p. 89)
The epigraph is from Cavafy's "Ithaka."
Kafenéion — Café.
Mezedes — Appetizers.
Sigá, sigá — Slowly, slowly.

—Stephen Davis

ALIKI BARNSTONE is a poet, translator, critic, and editor. Her books of poems are *Wild With It* (2002), a National Books Critics Circle Notable Book, *Madly in Love* (1997), *Windows in Providence* (1981), and *The Real Tin Flower* (which was introduced by Anne Sexton and was published in 1968, when she was twelve years old). She edited *A Book of Women Poets from Antiquity to Now* (1980; second edition, 1992), *The Calvinist Roots of the Modern Era* (1997), *The Shambhala Anthology of Women's Spiritual Poetry* (1999; 2003), and she introduced and wrote the readers' notes for H.D.'s *Trilogy* (1997). She has recorded a collaborative CD with musician Frank Haney. Her translation of C.P. Cavafy's collected poems and a study of the development of Emily Dickinson's poetry are forthcoming.

The daughter of poet, Willis Barnstone, and painter, Elli Tzalopoulou-Barnstone, Aliki was raised with her two brothers, Robert and Tony, in Bloomington, Indiana and Brandon, Vermont; the family traveled widely, especially to Greece, the country of her mother. Barnstone has also traveled to Spain, Holland, Italy, Portugal, England, Turkey, Mexico, Guatemala, Hong Kong, China, Tibet, Nepal, and Burma. She is married to fiction writer and visual artist, Joseph Clark; they have a daughter, Zoë. They live in Greece in the summer and Las Vegas in the winter. Barnstone currently teaches in the Creative Writing International Program at the University of Nevada, Las Vegas.